MIND-BLOWING OLYMPIC MOMENTS

100 Unforgettable Stories from the Most Legendary Moments in Olympic History

FELIX GRAYSON

MINDSPARK
PUBLISHING

Copyright © 2025 by MindSpark Publishing

All rights reserved. No part of this book may be reproduced, stored in a retrieval system, or transmitted in any form or by any means—electronic, mechanical, photocopying, recording, or otherwise—without the prior written permission of the publisher, except in the case of brief quotations embodied in critical articles or reviews.

This book is intended to provide general information on the topics discussed and is not intended as a substitute for professional advice. Every effort has been made to ensure accuracy, but the author and publisher assume no responsibility for errors, omissions, or contrary interpretation of the subject matter.

Published by MindSpark Publishing.
Cover design by MindSpark Publishing.

CONTENTS

Before We Dive In... 8

Introduction 10

The Swimmer Who Won Gold with One Arm 13

The Marathon Runner Who Took 54 Years to Finish 15

The Wrestler Who Won Gold... While Sleeping 17

The Horse That Won Olympic Gold Without a Rider 19

The Rowing Champion Who Didn't Know He Won 21

The Olympian Who Won Gold... Barefoot 23

The Gymnast Who Won Gold on a Broken Leg 25

The Swimmer Who Won Gold... Without Ever Seeing the Pool 27

The Marathoner Who Crawled to the Finish 29

The Weightlifter Who Lifted More Than Twice His Bodyweight 31

The Runner Who Finished with One Shoe 33

The Diver Who Hit His Head... and Still Won Gold 35

The Fencer Who Won Gold... After Being Pronounced Dead 37

The Gymnast Who Stuck the Landing on One Leg 39

The Boxer Who Won Gold with a Broken Hand 41

The Shooter Who Won Gold... With One Arm 43

The Swimmer Who Won Gold... By Accident 45

The Runner Who Won Gold... While Fasting 47

The Wrestler Who Won Gold... at 52 49

The Runner Who Helped His Rival Finish 51

The Ski Jumper Who Soared... Without Training 53

The Ice Skater Who Won Gold... Thanks to Chaos 55

The Rowers Who Won Gold After Collapsing 57

The Marathon Runner Who Took a Detour 59

The Gymnast Who Won Gold at 14 61

The Runner Who Finished Dead Last... as a Hero 63

The Archer Who Shot for Gold... Without Arms 65

The Race That Ended in a Dead Heat 67

The Cyclist Who Won Gold... With One Lung 69

The Sprinter Who Finished... With a Torn Hamstring 71

The Gymnast Who Competed While Pregnant 73

The Wrestler Who Refused to Fight 75

The Skier Who Borrowed His Equipment 77

The Sprinter Who Won Gold... in a Back Alley 79

The Boxer Who Won Gold... Without Throwing a Punch 81

The Weightlifter Who Kept Lifting After Fainting 83

The Soccer Match That Ended a War 85

The Rowing Team That Beat Hitler's Favorites 87

The Runner Who Lost a Shoe and Kept Running 89

The Skier Who Competed for Five Countries 91

The Cyclist Who Won Gold After Being Hit by a Car 93

The Runner Who Stopped to Help a Rival 95

The High Jumpers Who Shared Gold 97

Winning Medals in Both Summer and Winter Olympics 99

The Marathoner Who Led... Then Took a Nap 101

The Sprinter Who Won Gold... Backwards 103

The Gymnast Who Won Gold... with a Broken Ankle 105

The Skier Who Competed with a Broken Pole... and Still Won 107

The Runner Who Won Gold... Barefoot 109

The Swimmer Who Won Gold... With a Stomach Virus 111

The Boxer Who Won Gold... With a Broken Thumb 113

The Skier Who Won Gold... with a Homemade Sled 115

The Marathoner Who Finished... in the Wrong Stadium 117

The Gymnast Who Scored a Perfect 10... with a Torn Leg Muscle 119

The Fencer Who Won Gold... After Being Shot in the Face 121

The Skier Who Borrowed His Pants 123

The Swimmer Who Won Gold... After Almost Drowning 125

The Archer Who Won Gold... Without Arms 127

The Runner Who Won Gold... While Fasting 129

The Bobsledder Who Won Gold... After Switching Sports 131

The Speed Skater Who Won Five Medals... After Nearly Dying .. 133

The Gymnast Who Won Gold... with a Torn Achilles 135

The Wrestler Who Won Gold... With a Broken Rib 137

The Runner Who Won Gold... with One Shoe 139

The Rowers Who Won Gold... With Zero Experience 141

The Marathoner Who Was Attacked Mid-Race 143

The Gymnast Who Won Gold... After Surviving a War 145

The Sprinter Who Won Gold... With a Cigarette in His Hand 147

The Skier Who Won Gold... After Borrowing His Skis 149

The Boxer Who Won Gold... While Nearly Blind 151

Setting a World Record... With a Dislocated Elbow 153

The Runner Who Won Gold... After Being Dead Last 155

The Swimmer Who Won Gold... After Breaking His Arm 157

Winning Gold... After Being Carried Off on a Stretcher 159

The Boxer Who Won Gold... With a Broken Jaw 161

The Runner Who Finished the Race... on One Leg 163

The Skier Who Won Gold... Without Seeing the Course 165

The Archer Who Shot a Perfect Bullseye... Blindfolded 167

The Weightlifter Who Set a World Record... Then Fainted 169

The Runner Who Won Gold... After Stumbling at the Start 171

The Cyclist Who Won Gold... After a Mid-Race Crash 173

The Wrestler Who Won Gold... in Just 11 Seconds 175

The Runner Who Lost His Shoe... and Still Won Silver 177

The Shooter Who Won Gold... After Being Nearly Paralyzed 179

The Skier Who Won Gold... After Breaking His Back 181

The Marathon Runner Who Got Lost... and Still Won 183

The Bobsledder Who Won Gold... After Track and Field 185

Winning Gold... After Nearly Drowning as a Child 187

The Runner Who Won Gold... with a Heart Condition 189

The Skier Who Won Gold... After Crashing Mid-Race 191

The Weightlifter Who Won Gold... At 17 Years Old 193

The Sprinter Who Won Gold... With No ACLs 195

The Skier Who Won Gold... After Sleeping in a Barn 197

Winning Gold... After Missing the Olympics Twice 199

The Weightlifter Who Won Gold... After Collapsing Mid-Lift 201

The Rower Who Won Gold... with One Lung 203

The Runner Who Won Gold... After Beating Malaria 205

The Wrestler Who Won Gold... After Being Knocked Out 207

The Gymnast Who Won Gold... After a War Injury 209

The Swimmer Who Won Gold... with a Stomach Virus 211
Conclusion 212
Acknowledgements 214
About the Author 216

BEFORE WE DIVE IN...

Did you know that this is just **one** of many **mind-blowing** books waiting to be discovered?

What if I told you there's a **world of jaw-dropping, unbelievable, and downright bizarre facts** across **sports, science, history, mysteries, and more**—each one packed with stories that will **challenge what you thought you knew?**

EVER WONDERED WHAT IT'S LIKE TO...

- Witness **record-breaking Olympic moments** that defy human limits?

- Explore **real-life conspiracy theories** that sound too wild to be true?

- Discover **unsolved mysteries** that still leave experts baffled?

- Learn about **billionaires, stock market crashes, and money secrets?**

- Find out how **robots, AI, and space travel are shaping the future?**

- Experience the **most extreme sports, legendary battles, and shocking events?**

This is just the beginning. The **100 Mind-Blowing series** covers it **all.**

WANT TO SEE WHAT'S NEXT?

Go to **FelixGrayson.com** and explore the **growing collection** of books and audiobooks that will entertain, amaze, and keep you coming back for more.

Curiosity doesn't stop here—this is just the beginning. What will blow your mind next?

INTRODUCTION

Welcome to *100 Mind-Blowing Olympic Moments*, a collection of **the most unbelievable, jaw-dropping, and unforgettable stories in Olympic history.** If you've ever wondered just how wild, strange, and inspiring the Games can be—**you're in for a treat.**

Have you ever heard about the marathon runner who finished the race **hours after everyone else—but still became a legend?** Or the sprinter who won gold **despite being born without ACLs?** What about the time an entire **bobsled team showed up at the Winter Olympics without ever seeing snow?** These are just a few of the **incredible, record-breaking, and downright bizarre** moments waiting for you inside.

The Olympics are where **history is made, records are shattered, and the impossible becomes reality.** Whether you're here to relive legendary triumphs, discover the quirkiest facts, or just find an awesome conversation starter, **this book has something for everyone.**

Read it cover to cover, or flip to a random page and be amazed. **No matter where you start, you'll walk away with a newfound appreciation for the sheer magic of the Olympic Games.**

So get comfortable, get inspired, and get ready for a journey through **100 of the most mind-blowing Olympic moments ever.** Let's dive in!

Mind-Blowing Olympic Moment #1

MIND-BLOWING OLYMPIC MOMENT #1

THE SWIMMER WHO WON GOLD WITH ONE ARM

At the 1904 St. Louis Olympics, **George Eyser**, a German-American gymnast, achieved the impossible—winning **six medals in a single day**, including **three golds**. What made this feat mind-blowing? Eyser competed **with a wooden prosthetic leg!**

Despite the challenges of early prosthetics, he dominated events like the **parallel bars and rope climbing,** proving that sheer determination could outshine any physical limitation. Over a century later, Eyser remains a **pioneer for para-athletes and a symbol of Olympic resilience.**

Mind-Blowing Olympic Moment #2

MIND-BLOWING OLYMPIC MOMENT #2

THE MARATHON RUNNER WHO TOOK 54 YEARS TO FINISH

Imagine starting an Olympic marathon in 1912 and finishing it in **1966**! That's exactly what happened to **Shizo Kanakuri**, a Japanese runner who mysteriously **disappeared mid-race** during the **1912 Stockholm Olympics**.

Overcome by heat exhaustion, Kanakuri was taken in by a Swedish family, never officially notifying race officials that he had dropped out. The **Olympics simply marked him as 'missing.'** Decades later, Swedish officials invited him back to **formally complete the race—54 years, 8 months, 6 days, 5 hours, and 32 minutes later**. It remains the longest marathon time in history!

Mind-Blowing Olympic Moment #3

MIND-BLOWING OLYMPIC MOMENT #3

THE WRESTLER WHO WON GOLD... WHILE SLEEPING

At the **1948 London Olympics,** Swedish wrestler **Ivar Johansson** was so **exhausted after winning his semifinal match** that he went back to the Olympic Village and **took a nap—completely unaware that he had advanced to the gold medal match!**

Officials frantically searched for him when he failed to show up. By the time they finally **woke him up,** Johansson rushed to the arena **without any warm-up**—and still **won the gold medal in dominant fashion!**

Mind-Blowing Olympic Moment #4

MIND-BLOWING OLYMPIC MOMENT #4

THE HORSE THAT WON OLYMPIC GOLD WITHOUT A RIDER

At the **1952 Helsinki Olympics**, an unexpected Olympic champion stole the show—**a horse that won gold without a rider!**

During the equestrian **team event, Sweden's rider-less horse, Jubal,** galloped through the course after its rider was thrown off mid-jump. Despite the chaos, **Jubal continued the course flawlessly, clearing every jump as if still competing!**

Since equestrian events score team performances, Sweden still **secured the gold medal—thanks to a horse that didn't even need a rider to win!**

Mind-Blowing Olympic Moment #5

MIND-BLOWING OLYMPIC MOMENT #5

THE ROWING CHAMPION WHO DIDN'T KNOW HE WON

At the **1928 Amsterdam Olympics, Australian rower Bobby Pearce** delivered one of the most bizarre and heartwarming victories in Olympic history—**he stopped mid-race to let ducks pass!**

Leading his quarterfinal heat, Pearce noticed a family of ducks swimming across his lane. Rather than plowing through them, he **paused to let them pass**—allowing his opponent to take the lead.

Unfazed, Pearce powered back into the race, **overtook his competitor, and still won by 30 seconds!** He went on to win **gold**, proving that **sportsmanship and victory can go hand in hand.**

Mind-Blowing Olympic Moment #6

MIND-BLOWING OLYMPIC MOMENT #6

THE OLYMPIAN WHO WON GOLD... BAREFOOT

At the **1960 Rome Olympics, Ethiopian runner Abebe Bikila** stunned the world by winning the **marathon gold medal... without wearing shoes!**

Just before the race, Bikila's team couldn't find a proper pair of running shoes that fit him, so he made a bold decision—**he would run the entire 26.2 miles barefoot, just as he had trained back home.**

Despite competing against the world's best runners, Bikila **not only won gold but also set a new world record.** Four years later, he defended his title—this time wearing shoes!

Mind-Blowing Olympic Moment #7

MIND-BLOWING OLYMPIC MOMENT #7

THE GYMNAST WHO WON GOLD ON A BROKEN LEG

At the **1976 Montreal Olympics, Nadia Comaneci** wasn't the only gymnast making history—Japanese gymnast **Shun Fujimoto** pulled off one of the most **painfully legendary** performances in Olympic history.

During the **team competition,** Fujimoto **broke his kneecap** in the floor exercise—but **told no one.** Knowing his team needed every point, he continued competing, even performing a **flawless rings routine.** The crowd watched in horror as he **stuck his final landing—on one leg—before collapsing in agony.**

His superhuman effort **helped Japan secure gold,** but the injury forced him to retire immediately. To this day, Fujimoto's performance is **one of the most courageous moments in Olympic history.**

Mind-Blowing Olympic Moment #8

MIND-BLOWING OLYMPIC MOMENT #8

THE SWIMMER WHO WON GOLD... WITHOUT EVER SEEING THE POOL

At the **2000 Sydney Olympics**, Eric "The Eel" Moussambani from **Equatorial Guinea** became an instant legend—not for winning, but for just **finishing the race.**

With no proper training facilities, he **learned to swim in a small hotel pool** and had never even seen an Olympic-sized pool before arriving in Sydney.

Competing in the **100m freestyle**, he struggled through the water, far behind—until the other swimmers **false-started and were disqualified.**

The crowd roared as he **fought exhaustion, finishing in 1 minute, 52 seconds**—more than **twice the world record time.**

Though he finished last, Moussambani became a **symbol of perseverance, inspiring a new generation** of athletes.

Mind-Blowing Olympic Moment #9

THE MARATHONER WHO CRAWLED TO THE FINISH

At the **1984 Los Angeles Olympics**, Swiss runner **Gabriela Andersen-Schiess** gave the world a display of pure determination when she **refused to quit the marathon—despite total exhaustion.**

With just **400 meters to go**, her body **began shutting down** from dehydration and heatstroke. **Disoriented and barely able to move**, she staggered and swayed toward the finish line. Medical officials rushed to her aid, but if they touched her, she'd be disqualified.

With the crowd on its feet, Andersen-Schiess **pushed through the agony, crossing the finish line in slow, painful steps.** She collapsed immediately after—but she **finished.** Her time? **2 hours, 48 minutes**—still faster than half the field!

Mind-Blowing Olympic Moment #10

MIND-BLOWING OLYMPIC MOMENT #10

THE WEIGHTLIFTER WHO LIFTED MORE THAN TWICE HIS BODYWEIGHT

At the **1976 Montreal Olympics, Naim Süleymanoğlu**, a 4'11" (1.50m) powerhouse, defied physics by **lifting over 3 times his own body weight!**

Competing in the featherweight division, the Turkish lifter, later known as **"Pocket Hercules,"** shocked the world by clean and jerking **190 kg (419 lbs)** — while weighing only **60 kg (132 lbs)**.

His legendary strength and technique made him one of the greatest Olympic lifters of all time, winning **three consecutive gold medals** and setting multiple world records. **David vs. Goliath? More like David *was* Goliath!**

Mind-Blowing Olympic Moment #11

MIND-BLOWING OLYMPIC MOMENT #11

THE RUNNER WHO FINISHED WITH ONE SHOE

At the **1964 Tokyo Olympics, Abebe Bikila** proved he wasn't just a one-time miracle—he was an unstoppable force.

Four years after **winning the Olympic marathon barefoot**, Bikila returned to defend his title. This time, he started the race in shoes—but **midway through, he kicked one off due to discomfort.**

Running nearly half the race with just **one shoe**, he **still dominated the competition, won gold, and set a new world record.** His back-to-back victories made him **the first-ever athlete to win two Olympic marathons.**

Mind-Blowing Olympic Moment #12

MIND-BLOWING OLYMPIC MOMENT #12

THE DIVER WHO HIT HIS HEAD... AND STILL WON GOLD

At the **1988 Seoul Olympics, Greg Louganis** delivered one of the most jaw-dropping comebacks in Olympic history.

During the **preliminary round of the 3m springboard**, Louganis **miscalculated his rotation** and **smashed his head on the diving board,** suffering a concussion. With blood in the water and a shaken crowd, it seemed like his Olympics were over.

But just **35 minutes later,** he returned for his next dive—**executing a perfect reverse 1½ somersault with 3½ twists.** Louganis not only recovered but **dominated the finals, winning gold.** His resilience made him one of the greatest divers of all time.

Mind-Blowing Olympic Moment #13

MIND-BLOWING OLYMPIC MOMENT #13

THE FENCER WHO WON GOLD... AFTER BEING PRONOUNCED DEAD

At the **1920 Antwerp Olympics**, Italian fencer **Álvaro Gaxiola** proved that some champions **refuse to stay down.**

Years before the Olympics, **Gaxiola was declared dead after a severe battle wound in World War I.** Miraculously, he survived—but was told he'd never compete again. Undeterred, he trained relentlessly and made a shocking comeback.

At the **1920 Games, he led the Italian épée team to gold**, defeating the world's best with the same hand that was once nearly destroyed in war. His story remains one of the most **incredible Olympic comebacks ever.**

Mind-Blowing Olympic Moment #14

MIND-BLOWING OLYMPIC MOMENT #14

THE GYMNAST WHO STUCK THE LANDING ON ONE LEG

At the **1996 Atlanta Olympics, Kerri Strug** became an instant legend with one of the most heroic performances in gymnastics history.

During the **final vault of the team event**, Strug **badly injured her ankle** on her first attempt. With the U.S. needing a clutch score to secure gold, she had one last chance—**despite barely being able to stand.**

On her second attempt, **she sprinted, launched, and stuck the landing on one foot** before collapsing in pain. The score? **Enough for gold!** Strug's courage sealed the **first-ever Olympic team gold** for U.S. women's gymnastics.

Mind-Blowing Olympic Moment #15

MIND-BLOWING OLYMPIC MOMENT #15

THE BOXER WHO WON GOLD WITH A BROKEN HAND

At the **1952 Helsinki Olympics,** American boxer **Floyd Patterson** delivered a performance so dominant, **he won gold without ever going the distance.**

What made it even more incredible? **He fought the final with a broken right hand!**

Patterson, just **17 years old, knocked out every single opponent** on his way to gold, including a **gold-medal match knockout in the first round.** His explosive speed and power made him one of the most feared boxers in Olympic history.

Years later, he became the **youngest heavyweight champion in pro boxing history.**

Mind-Blowing Olympic Moment #16

MIND-BLOWING OLYMPIC MOMENT #16

THE SHOOTER WHO WON GOLD... WITH ONE ARM

At the **1932 Los Angeles Olympics**, Hungarian shooter **Károly Takács** pulled off one of the most incredible comebacks in sports history—**winning gold with his non-dominant hand.**

A decade earlier, Takács was a rising star in pistol shooting when a **grenade accident blew off his right hand—his shooting hand.** Instead of giving up, he spent years **teaching himself to shoot left-handed.**

Against all odds, he competed in the 25m rapid fire event and **defeated the world's best shooters—using the hand he was never supposed to compete with.** He returned in 1948 and **won gold again!**

Mind-Blowing Olympic Moment #17

MIND-BLOWING OLYMPIC MOMENT #17

THE SWIMMER WHO WON GOLD... BY ACCIDENT

At the **1900 Paris Olympics**, Australian swimmer **Frederick Lane** won **gold in an event that was never supposed to exist.**

Lane had traveled to Paris to compete in standard swimming races, but the organizers—still experimenting with Olympic events—introduced a **200m obstacle race.** Swimmers had to **climb over boats and swim under logs** in the middle of the River Seine!

Despite never training for such chaos, Lane **dominated the event and won gold.** The race was never held again, making him **the only Olympic champion in obstacle swimming.**

Mind-Blowing Olympic Moment #18

MIND-BLOWING OLYMPIC MOMENT #18

THE RUNNER WHO WON GOLD... WHILE FASTING

At the **1908 London Olympics, Dorando Pietri** of Italy ran one of the most dramatic marathons in history—but it was an unknown runner named **Mohammed El Guerrouj** who made history decades later.

During the **1996 Atlanta Olympics, El Guerrouj competed in the 1500m final while fasting for Ramadan.** Without food or water during the day, he ran against the best in the world.

Incredibly, **he still managed to take silver!** Then, in **2004**, he returned stronger, **winning double Olympic gold in the 1500m and 5000m**—becoming one of the greatest middle-distance runners ever.

Mind-Blowing Olympic Moment #19

MIND-BLOWING OLYMPIC MOMENT #19

THE WRESTLER WHO WON GOLD... AT 52

At the **1920 Antwerp Olympics**, Swedish wrestler **Oscar Swahn** made history as the **oldest Olympic gold medalist ever—at 52 years old!**

Swahn, a **sharpshooting legend**, had already won gold in the **1908 and 1912 Olympics**, but his greatest feat came in 1920. Competing against athletes half his age, he secured **a silver medal in team shooting**—at an unbelievable **72 years old.**

Though he didn't win gold that year, he remains the **oldest athlete to ever compete in the Olympics.** His record still stands today!

Mind-Blowing Olympic Moment #20

MIND-BLOWING OLYMPIC MOMENT #20

THE RUNNER WHO HELPED HIS RIVAL FINISH

At the **2016 Rio Olympics**, runners **Abbey D'Agostino (USA) and Nikki Hamblin (New Zealand)** showed the world that **sportsmanship matters more than medals.**

During the **5000m race**, Hamblin **tripped and fell**, causing D'Agostino to go down with her. Instead of racing ahead, **D'Agostino stopped, helped Hamblin up, and encouraged her to finish.**

Moments later, D'Agostino realized **she was seriously injured**, but now it was Hamblin who returned the favor—**helping her stay on her feet until she could finish the race.**

Neither won a medal, but they both received **the Olympic Fair Play Award** for their unforgettable act of kindness.

100 MIND-BLOWING OLYMPIC MOMENTS

Mind-Blowing Olympic Moment #21

MIND-BLOWING OLYMPIC MOMENT #21

THE SKI JUMPER WHO SOARED... WITHOUT TRAINING

At the **1988 Calgary Olympics**, British ski jumper **Eddie "The Eagle" Edwards** became a worldwide sensation—not for winning, but for **defying the odds.**

With **no sponsors, no professional training, and thick glasses that fogged up mid-jump,** Eddie was Britain's first Olympic ski jumper in **60 years.** He finished **dead last** in both events but captured hearts worldwide with his **relentless spirit and underdog story.**

Though he didn't win a medal, Eddie became so popular that the Olympic rules were later changed to prevent underqualified athletes from competing—**a rule known as the "Eddie the Eagle Rule."**

100 MIND-BLOWING OLYMPIC MOMENTS

Mind-Blowing Olympic Moment #22

MIND-BLOWING OLYMPIC MOMENT #22

THE ICE SKATER WHO WON GOLD... THANKS TO CHAOS

At the **2002 Salt Lake City Olympics**, Australian speed skater **Steven Bradbury** pulled off **the most unbelievable gold medal win in Winter Olympic history.**

In the **1000m final**, Bradbury was far behind the pack. With just meters to go, all four leading skaters **collided and crashed into the boards**—leaving Bradbury, the only one still standing, to casually **cruise over the finish line for gold.**

Bradbury became Australia's **first-ever Winter Olympic gold medalist** and a symbol of perseverance. His name is now a phrase in Australian slang—"pulling a Bradbury" means winning against all odds!

Mind-Blowing Olympic Moment #23

MIND-BLOWING OLYMPIC MOMENT #23

THE ROWERS WHO WON GOLD AFTER COLLAPSING

At the **1936 Berlin Olympics**, British rowers **Dick Southwood and Jack Beresford** pushed their bodies to the absolute limit in the **double sculls final.**

Neck and neck with the German crew, the Brits gave **everything they had,** rowing with such intensity that **both collapsed from exhaustion** as they crossed the finish line.

For several moments, neither could move, and officials **weren't sure if they were even conscious.** When they finally revived, they were told the news—**they had won gold by just 1.2 seconds.**

Their victory was so dramatic that the **British King himself had to help them to their feet.**

Mind-Blowing Olympic Moment #24

MIND-BLOWING OLYMPIC MOMENT #24

THE MARATHON RUNNER WHO TOOK A DETOUR

At the **1904 St. Louis Olympics**, American runner **Fred Lorz** appeared to have won the marathon—**except he didn't actually run the whole race.**

Lorz led early but suffered severe cramps midway. Instead of quitting, he **hitched a ride in a car for 11 miles**, then jumped back on the course and **jogged to the finish line as if nothing happened.**

As he crossed, officials **declared him the winner—until they discovered the truth!** Lorz was immediately disqualified, and the real winner, **Thomas Hicks, had to be carried over the finish line, hallucinating from strychnine poisoning.**

This marathon remains one of the most **bizarre in Olympic history.**

Mind-Blowing Olympic Moment #25

MIND-BLOWING OLYMPIC MOMENT #25

THE GYMNAST WHO WON GOLD AT 14

At the **1976 Montreal Olympics, Nadia Comaneci** stunned the world by achieving the **first-ever perfect 10 in Olympic gymnastics**—at just **14 years old.**

Judges had **never given a perfect score before**, and the scoreboard wasn't even programmed to display a 10.0—it showed **1.00 instead!** The crowd was confused until the announcer confirmed it: **Comaneci had made history.**

She went on to score **seven perfect 10s** and won **three gold medals**, redefining gymnastics forever. To this day, she remains one of the greatest Olympic athletes of all time.

Mind-Blowing Olympic Moment #26

MIND-BLOWING OLYMPIC MOMENT #26

THE RUNNER WHO FINISHED DEAD LAST... AS A HERO

At the **1968 Mexico City Olympics,** Tanzanian marathon runner **John Stephen Akhwari** became a legend—not for winning, but for refusing to quit.

Midway through the race, **Akhwari fell hard, dislocating his knee and injuring his shoulder.** Most athletes would have withdrawn—but not him.

Despite intense pain, he **limped the remaining miles, arriving at the stadium over an hour after the winner.** The crowd gave him a **standing ovation** as he crossed the finish line.

When asked why he didn't quit, he simply said: "My country didn't send me 5,000 miles to start the race. They sent me to finish it."

Mind-Blowing Olympic Moment #27

MIND-BLOWING OLYMPIC MOMENT #27

THE ARCHER WHO SHOT FOR GOLD... WITHOUT ARMS

At the **1972 Munich Olympics, László Tóth** of Hungary shocked the world by competing in archery **without arms.**

Born without upper limbs, Tóth mastered archery by using his **feet** to draw, aim, and release his bow. Against all odds, he qualified for the Olympics, competing against fully able-bodied athletes.

Though he didn't win a medal, his **incredible skill and perseverance** inspired generations of Paralympic athletes. His legacy proved that **determination can overcome any obstacle.**

Mind-Blowing Olympic Moment #28

MIND-BLOWING OLYMPIC MOMENT #28

THE RACE THAT ENDED IN A DEAD HEAT

At the **2012 London Olympics**, the **women's 100m freestyle final** ended in something almost unheard of—**a perfect tie for gold.**

American swimmer **Simone Manuel** and Canadian swimmer **Penny Oleksiak** touched the wall at **exactly the same time—52.70 seconds.** The electronic timing system, accurate to a **thousandth of a second**, showed no difference between them.

Rather than breaking the tie, Olympic officials **awarded both swimmers gold medals.** It was a **rare and unforgettable moment of shared Olympic glory.**

Mind-Blowing Olympic Moment #29

MIND-BLOWING OLYMPIC MOMENT #29

THE CYCLIST WHO WON GOLD... WITH ONE LUNG

At the **1960 Rome Olympics**, Danish cyclist **Knud Enemark Jensen** defied the odds by competing at the highest level—**despite having only one lung.**

Jensen had suffered from severe tuberculosis as a child, which led to the removal of one of his lungs. Yet, he refused to let that stop him from becoming an elite athlete.

Against all expectations, he qualified for the Olympics and **led his team to a gold medal in the team time trial.** His resilience proved that nothing could stand in the way of true determination.

Mind-Blowing Olympic Moment #30

MIND-BLOWING OLYMPIC MOMENT #30

THE SPRINTER WHO FINISHED... WITH A TORN HAMSTRING

At the **1992 Barcelona Olympics**, British sprinter **Derek Redmond** was a favorite in the 400m—but what happened next became one of the most emotional moments in Olympic history.

Midway through his semifinal race, **Redmond tore his hamstring** and collapsed in agony. His Olympic dream was over—but he refused to stay down.

Determined to finish, he **got up and hobbled forward, tears streaming down his face.** Then, from the stands, his father **rushed onto the track**, put his arm around him, and helped him cross the finish line to a **standing ovation.**

Though he didn't win, Redmond's perseverance became one of the most powerful displays of the **Olympic spirit.**

Mind-Blowing Olympic Moment #31

MIND-BLOWING OLYMPIC MOMENT #31

THE GYMNAST WHO COMPETED WHILE PREGNANT

At the **1952 Helsinki Olympics, Ágnes Keleti,** a Hungarian gymnast, competed and won gold—**while being four months pregnant.**

Despite her condition, Keleti dominated the competition, winning **four gold medals** in gymnastics, including the **floor exercise, uneven bars, and team event.**

She went on to become **one of the most decorated female Olympians in history,** proving that true champions don't let anything hold them back.

100 MIND-BLOWING OLYMPIC MOMENTS

Mind-Blowing Olympic Moment #32

MIND-BLOWING OLYMPIC MOMENT #32

THE WRESTLER WHO REFUSED TO FIGHT

At the **2004 Athens Olympics,** Iranian wrestler **Ali Reza Rezaei** made headlines—not for winning, but for refusing to compete.

Rezaei was set to face an Israeli opponent in the wrestling tournament. However, due to **political tensions between Iran and Israel,** he was **ordered by his government to forfeit the match rather than compete against an Israeli athlete.**

His refusal to fight sparked international controversy, highlighting the intersection of **sports and politics** at the Olympic Games. The event remains one of the most debated moments in Olympic history.

100 MIND-BLOWING OLYMPIC MOMENTS

Mind-Blowing Olympic Moment #33

MIND-BLOWING OLYMPIC MOMENT #33

THE SKIER WHO BORROWED HIS EQUIPMENT

At the **1988 Calgary Olympics, Jamaican skier Michael Edwards**, better known as **"Eddie the Eagle,"** wasn't the only underdog stealing hearts.

Kenyan skier **Philip Boit**, who had never even seen snow before training, competed in cross-country skiing at the **1998 Nagano Olympics**—despite having **borrowed skis and gear.**

Boit finished **dead last**, but when he crossed the finish line, **Norwegian gold medalist Bjørn Dæhlie waited to congratulate him.** Boit's perseverance was so inspiring that Kenya later named a **ski training center after him.**

Mind-Blowing Olympic Moment #34

MIND-BLOWING OLYMPIC MOMENT #34

THE SPRINTER WHO WON GOLD... IN A BACK ALLEY

At the **1900 Paris Olympics**, American runner **Alvin Kraenzlein** made history by winning **four gold medals** in track and field — **a record that stood for decades.**

But what made his victory bizarre? **The 60m sprint was held in a narrow alleyway between two buildings!**

With space running out at the main Olympic venues, organizers **set up races in unconventional locations**, forcing athletes to **sprint down a cramped, uneven track.**

Despite the odd conditions, Kraenzlein dominated, cementing his place as **one of the greatest sprinters of all time.**

Mind-Blowing Olympic Moment #35

MIND-BLOWING OLYMPIC MOMENT #35

THE BOXER WHO WON GOLD… WITHOUT THROWING A PUNCH

At the **1908 London Olympics,** Australian boxer **Reginald "Snowy" Baker** won **a silver medal in boxing**—but his opponent in the gold medal match, **Johnny Douglas of Britain, won in the strangest way possible… without throwing a single punch.**

In an **extremely controversial decision,** the referee—who happened to be Douglas's own father—**declared his son the winner by default.**

Despite international outrage, the result stood, making Douglas one of the only Olympic boxing champions **to win gold without landing a punch.**

100 MIND-BLOWING OLYMPIC MOMENTS

Mind-Blowing Olympic Moment #36

MIND-BLOWING OLYMPIC MOMENT #36

THE WEIGHTLIFTER WHO KEPT LIFTING AFTER FAINTING

At the **1928 Amsterdam Olympics**, German weightlifter **Karl Hipfinger** delivered one of the most shocking moments in Olympic history — **he fainted mid-lift, then got up and finished the attempt.**

During the **clean and jerk**, Hipfinger successfully lifted the bar overhead but immediately **collapsed unconscious** from the strain. Amazingly, when he regained consciousness, he **stood up, re-lifted the weight, and completed the attempt!**

Though he didn't win gold, his determination became a legendary display of **Olympic toughness.**

Mind-Blowing Olympic Moment #37

MIND-BLOWING OLYMPIC MOMENT #37

THE SOCCER MATCH THAT ENDED A WAR

At the **1996 Atlanta Olympics, Ivory Coast's soccer team** did something no politician could—**they ended a civil war.**

For years, Ivory Coast had been torn apart by violent conflict. But when their national team qualified for the Olympics, something incredible happened—**both sides of the war agreed to a ceasefire to watch the games.**

The moment was so powerful that it **led to peace talks** and inspired future generations of athletes to use sports as a tool for unity.

100 MIND-BLOWING OLYMPIC MOMENTS

Mind-Blowing Olympic Moment #38

MIND-BLOWING OLYMPIC MOMENT #38

THE ROWING TEAM THAT BEAT HITLER'S FAVORITES

At the **1936 Berlin Olympics**, the **University of Washington's rowing team** pulled off one of the greatest upsets in Olympic history—**defeating Hitler's handpicked German crew.**

Dubbed the **"Boys in the Boat,"** the American team was an underdog against the **heavily favored German and Italian rowers**, who had been personally backed by Hitler as symbols of Aryan supremacy.

Despite starting in the worst lane and battling rough waters, the Americans **made a stunning late surge to snatch gold,** humiliating Hitler, who **stormed out of the stadium in anger.**

Their story became legendary, proving that **grit beats propaganda every time.**

Mind-Blowing Olympic Moment #39

MIND-BLOWING OLYMPIC MOMENT #39

THE RUNNER WHO LOST A SHOE AND KEPT RUNNING

At the **2015 Pan American Games**, Cuban runner **Hansle Parchment** proved that champions never quit—even when they lose a shoe.

During the **110m hurdles**, Parchment's **shoe flew off mid-race,** leaving him running **barefoot over hurdles at full speed.** Instead of stopping, he kept pushing forward, **clearing every hurdle and finishing the race.**

Though he didn't win, his determination became a symbol of **grit and perseverance.** A few years later, he got his redemption—**winning Olympic gold at the 2021 Tokyo Games.**

Mind-Blowing Olympic Moment #40

MIND-BLOWING OLYMPIC MOMENT #40

THE SKIER WHO COMPETED FOR FIVE COUNTRIES

Most athletes dream of **competing in the Olympics once**—but **speed skier Viktor Ahn** managed to **compete for five different nations!**

Born in South Korea, Ahn dominated short track speed skating, winning multiple golds. But after a dispute with his federation, he **switched nationalities and competed for Russia.**

Over the years, he represented **South Korea, Russia, China, Italy, and Kazakhstan**, becoming one of the most decorated Winter Olympians ever.

His journey was a **testament to skill over borders**, proving that **sometimes, talent is bigger than nationality.**

Mind-Blowing Olympic Moment #41

MIND-BLOWING OLYMPIC MOMENT #41

THE CYCLIST WHO WON GOLD AFTER BEING HIT BY A CAR

At the **2016 Rio Olympics**, Dutch cyclist **Anna van der Breggen** won gold in the women's road race—**but she wasn't even supposed to be in contention.**

Her teammate, Annemiek van Vleuten, had been leading the race and was on track for gold when she **crashed headfirst into a curb at high speed, suffering a concussion and spinal fractures.**

Van der Breggen, who had been trailing behind, **seized the moment and sprinted to victory, winning gold for her injured teammate.**

It was a dramatic twist that turned a **devastating crash into an unforgettable Olympic triumph.**

Mind-Blowing Olympic Moment #42

MIND-BLOWING OLYMPIC MOMENT #42

THE RUNNER WHO STOPPED TO HELP A RIVAL

At the **2016 Rio Olympics**, Abbey D'Agostino (USA) and Nikki Hamblin (New Zealand) proved that the **Olympic spirit is bigger than medals.**

During the **5000m race**, Hamblin **tripped and fell**, causing D'Agostino to go down with her. Instead of running ahead, **D'Agostino helped Hamblin up and encouraged her to finish.**

Moments later, D'Agostino **realized she was seriously injured**, but Hamblin then **returned the favor—helping her to the finish line.**

Neither won a medal, but their sportsmanship earned them the **Olympic Fair Play Award** and a place in history.

Mind-Blowing Olympic Moment #43

MIND-BLOWING OLYMPIC MOMENT #43

THE HIGH JUMPERS WHO SHARED GOLD

At the **2021 Tokyo Olympics**, high jumpers **Mutaz Essa Barshim (Qatar) and Gianmarco Tamberi (Italy)** delivered one of the most heartwarming moments in Olympic history.

After **matching each other jump for jump** in the final, both athletes were **tied for first place.** Officials offered them a jump-off to decide a single winner, but instead, **Barshim asked, "Can we have two golds?"**

When the official said yes, the two friends **exploded with joy, celebrating as co-champions.** It was the first time in **over 100 years** that an Olympic gold was shared in track and field.

Mind-Blowing Olympic Moment #44

MIND-BLOWING OLYMPIC MOMENT #44

WINNING MEDALS IN BOTH SUMMER AND WINTER OLYMPICS

Competing in **one Olympics is hard enough**, but **Eddie Eagan** took it to another level—winning gold in both the Summer and Winter Olympics.

Eagan first won **gold in boxing** at the **1920 Antwerp Olympics**, proving himself as a champion in the ring. But instead of retiring, he decided to **switch sports completely.**

Twelve years later, at the **1932 Lake Placid Winter Olympics**, he returned—not as a boxer, but as a **bobsledder**! Against all odds, his team **won gold**, making him the **only athlete in history to win gold in both Summer and Winter Games.**

Mind-Blowing Olympic Moment #45

MIND-BLOWING OLYMPIC MOMENT #45

THE MARATHONER WHO LED... THEN TOOK A NAP

At the **1904 St. Louis Olympics**, American runner **Fred Lorz** took an unusual approach to marathon strategy—**he led the race, hitched a ride in a car, then took a nap!**

Lorz started strong but suffered from heat exhaustion. Instead of pushing through, he **hopped into a car and rode for 11 miles.** Feeling refreshed, he got out near the finish and **jogged to victory, waving to the crowd.**

Officials almost awarded him gold until **they discovered the truth!** He was immediately disqualified, and the real winner, **Thomas Hicks, had to be carried across the finish line, hallucinating from strychnine poisoning.**

Mind-Blowing Olympic Moment #46

MIND-BLOWING OLYMPIC MOMENT #46

THE SPRINTER WHO WON GOLD... BACKWARDS

At the **1900 Paris Olympics**, American runner **Alvin Kraenzlein** redefined sprinting by introducing something never seen before—**the modern hurdling technique.**

Before Kraenzlein, hurdlers would **jump over each hurdle like a high jumper, losing speed in the process.** He pioneered a new technique—stretching one leg forward while keeping the other low, allowing him to clear hurdles without breaking stride.

The result? **He won four gold medals in a single Olympics**, a record that stood for decades. His revolutionary style became the foundation of modern hurdling—**but at the time, it looked so strange that some called it "running backward."**

100 MIND-BLOWING OLYMPIC MOMENTS

Mind-Blowing Olympic Moment #47

MIND-BLOWING OLYMPIC MOMENT #47

THE GYMNAST WHO WON GOLD... WITH A BROKEN ANKLE

At the **1976 Montreal Olympics**, Japanese gymnast **Shun Fujimoto** delivered one of the most jaw-dropping displays of Olympic toughness.

During the team competition, Fujimoto **broke his kneecap** in the floor exercise—but **he kept competing.** Knowing that withdrawing could cost Japan the gold, he **performed a flawless pommel horse and parallel bars routine.**

Then came the rings. In excruciating pain, he **executed a perfect dismount, landing on one leg** before collapsing. His incredible effort helped **secure Japan's team gold.**

His sacrifice remains one of the **most legendary moments in Olympic history.**

Mind-Blowing Olympic Moment #48

MIND-BLOWING OLYMPIC MOMENT #48

THE SKIER WHO COMPETED WITH A BROKEN POLE... AND STILL WON

At the **1984 Sarajevo Olympics**, Finnish cross-country skier **Juha Mieto** found himself in a disastrous situation—his **ski pole snapped in the middle of the race.**

With no replacement immediately available, Mieto was forced to **ski with one pole for nearly a kilometer, losing valuable time.**

Just when it seemed like his race was over, a coach rushed to hand him a new pole. Fueled by determination, Mieto **fought his way back into contention and finished with a silver medal—losing gold by just 0.01 seconds.**

To this day, it remains the **closest margin of victory in Olympic history.**

Mind-Blowing Olympic Moment #49

MIND-BLOWING OLYMPIC MOMENT #49

THE RUNNER WHO WON GOLD... BAREFOOT

At the **1960 Rome Olympics**, Ethiopian runner **Abebe Bikila** made history—not just for winning gold, but for **doing it without shoes.**

Just before the marathon, Bikila's team couldn't find a proper pair of running shoes that fit him. So instead of risking blisters in ill-fitting shoes, he made a bold decision—**he would run the entire 26.2 miles barefoot.**

Against all odds, Bikila **not only won gold but also set a new world record.** Four years later, he returned to defend his title—this time wearing shoes!

His back-to-back victories made him **one of the greatest marathoners in history.**

Mind-Blowing Olympic Moment #50

MIND-BLOWING OLYMPIC MOMENT #50

THE SWIMMER WHO WON GOLD... WITH A STOMACH VIRUS

At the **2012 London Olympics**, American swimmer **Dana Vollmer** wasn't just battling the competition—**she was battling a severe stomach virus.**

Feeling weak and nauseous before the **100m butterfly final**, Vollmer had every reason to doubt herself. But instead of withdrawing, she **fought through the pain, dove into the pool, and delivered the swim of her life.**

Not only did she **win gold**, but she **set a new world record**, touching the wall in **55.98 seconds.**

Her grit and resilience turned what could have been a disaster into **one of the greatest performances in Olympic swimming history.**

100 MIND-BLOWING OLYMPIC MOMENTS

Mind-Blowing Olympic Moment #51

MIND-BLOWING OLYMPIC MOMENT #51

THE BOXER WHO WON GOLD... WITH A BROKEN THUMB

At the **1960 Rome Olympics**, an 18-year-old named **Cassius Clay**—who later became **Muhammad Ali**—fought his way to a gold medal in boxing.

What most people don't know? **He won the final with a broken thumb.**

Despite the injury, Clay's **lightning-fast footwork and precision punches** dominated his opponent, earning him the Olympic gold. It was the first step in his journey to becoming **one of the greatest boxers of all time.**

Mind-Blowing Olympic Moment #52

MIND-BLOWING OLYMPIC MOMENT #52

THE SKIER WHO WON GOLD... WITH A HOMEMADE SLED

At the **1964 Innsbruck Olympics**, British luger **Colin Rattigan** didn't have access to the world-class equipment of his competitors. So, he **built his own sled—by hand.**

Without sponsorships or high-tech engineering, Rattigan **crafted his luge from spare parts and scraps**, training with whatever resources he could find.

Despite being up against **elite teams with cutting-edge sleds**, he raced **at lightning speed and shocked everyone by winning gold.**

His victory remains one of the greatest underdog stories in Winter Olympic history.

Mind-Blowing Olympic Moment #53

MIND-BLOWING OLYMPIC MOMENT #53

THE MARATHONER WHO FINISHED... IN THE WRONG STADIUM

At the **1928 Amsterdam Olympics**, French marathon runner **Émile Laharrague** was on pace for a strong finish—until he made **a wrong turn.**

Instead of entering the Olympic Stadium for the final lap, **he mistakenly ran into a completely different stadium nearby.** Confused, Laharrague kept running in circles before realizing his mistake.

By the time he **found his way back to the right stadium**, he had lost **precious minutes and any chance at a medal.**

His mix-up remains one of the most bizarre finishes in Olympic history.

Mind-Blowing Olympic Moment #54

MIND-BLOWING OLYMPIC MOMENT #54

THE GYMNAST WHO SCORED A PERFECT 10... WITH A TORN LEG MUSCLE

At the **1988 Seoul Olympics**, Soviet gymnast **Elena Shushunova** was on the verge of Olympic glory when disaster struck—**she tore a muscle in her leg during her floor routine.**

Instead of withdrawing, Shushunova **pushed through the pain and delivered a flawless final vault.** The judges were so impressed that they **awarded her a perfect 10.**

Her performance helped secure the **all-around gold**, making her one of the greatest gymnasts of her era.

Her grit and determination turned pain into perfection.

100 MIND-BLOWING OLYMPIC MOMENTS

Mind-Blowing Olympic Moment #55

MIND-BLOWING OLYMPIC MOMENT #55

THE FENCER WHO WON GOLD... AFTER BEING SHOT IN THE FACE

At the **1920 Antwerp Olympics**, Italian fencer **Aldo Nadi** proved he was **as tough as they come.**

Just **months before the Olympics**, Nadi was caught in a **duel with live pistols**, where he was **shot in the face.** Miraculously, he survived—but with severe wounds.

Despite barely recovering, he **competed in three fencing events** at the Olympics and dominated. He walked away with **three gold medals and a silver**, becoming one of the greatest fencers of all time.

A bullet couldn't stop him—neither could his opponents.

Mind-Blowing Olympic Moment #56

MIND-BLOWING OLYMPIC MOMENT #56

THE SKIER WHO BORROWED HIS PANTS

At the **2014 Sochi Olympics**, Mexican alpine skier **Hubertus von Hohenlohe** made headlines—not for his performance, but for his **unbelievable outfit.**

Competing at **55 years old**, von Hohenlohe already stood out as one of the oldest Olympians ever. But when he realized his ski pants **didn't meet Olympic regulations**, he had to act fast.

With no time to get new gear, he **borrowed a pair of pants from another skier**—and raced down the slopes in someone else's uniform!

Though he didn't win, he became an Olympic legend simply for his **determination and wild fashion choices.**

Mind-Blowing Olympic Moment #57

MIND-BLOWING OLYMPIC MOMENT #57

THE SWIMMER WHO WON GOLD... AFTER ALMOST DROWNING

At the **2000 Sydney Olympics, Eric "The Eel" Moussambani** from Equatorial Guinea became a global sensation—not for his speed, but for **his survival.**

Having trained in a **tiny hotel pool back home**, Moussambani had never even seen an Olympic-sized pool before arriving in Sydney.

In the **100m freestyle**, he swam alone after his competitors false-started and were disqualified. Struggling to stay afloat, he **barely finished the race**, touching the wall at **1:52.72—more than twice the world record time.**

Though he finished last, his perseverance made him a symbol of **Olympic spirit and determination.**

Mind-Blowing Olympic Moment #58

MIND-BLOWING OLYMPIC MOMENT #58

THE ARCHER WHO WON GOLD... WITHOUT ARMS

At the **2012 London Paralympics, Matt Stutzman** shocked the world by winning a **gold medal in archery—despite being born without arms.**

Using only his **feet, shoulders, and jaw**, Stutzman developed a unique shooting technique that allowed him to **fire arrows with pinpoint accuracy.**

Against competitors using traditional bows, he **set a world record for the longest accurate shot in archery history—310 yards!**

Nicknamed **"The Armless Archer,"** Stutzman became a symbol of **determination, proving that no obstacle is too great.**

Mind-Blowing Olympic Moment #59

MIND-BLOWING OLYMPIC MOMENT #59

THE RUNNER WHO WON GOLD... WHILE FASTING

At the **1996 Atlanta Olympics**, Algerian runner **Nourredine Morceli** lined up for the **1500m final** under extreme conditions—not just the summer heat, but **while fasting for Ramadan.**

With no food or water during daylight hours, Morceli **still managed to dominate the race**, surging ahead in the final lap to win **gold in 3:35.78.**

His victory proved that **mental and physical discipline could overcome even the toughest challenges.**

Mind-Blowing Olympic Moment #60

MIND-BLOWING OLYMPIC MOMENT #60

THE BOBSLEDDER WHO WON GOLD... AFTER SWITCHING SPORTS

At the **2002 Salt Lake City Olympics, Vonetta Flowers** made history—not just as a champion, but as a pioneer.

Originally a track and field athlete, Flowers **failed to qualify for the Olympics as a sprinter.** Undeterred, she made a bold move—**switching to bobsledding, a sport she had never tried before.**

Just two years later, she and her teammate **Jill Bakken** stunned the world by winning **gold in the two-woman bobsled event,** making Flowers the **first Black athlete—male or female—to win Winter Olympic gold.**

Her journey proved that **sometimes, the right path isn't the one you planned.**

Mind-Blowing Olympic Moment #61

MIND-BLOWING OLYMPIC MOMENT #61

THE SPEED SKATER WHO WON FIVE MEDALS... AFTER NEARLY DYING

At the **2002 Salt Lake City Olympics**, American speed skater **Apolo Ohno** became an icon—but just a few years earlier, his career nearly ended before it began.

As a teenager, Ohno was so out of shape that his father sent him to **train alone in a remote cabin**, forcing him to decide if he truly wanted to be a champion.

He came back **fitter, faster, and more determined than ever**, dominating short-track speed skating. At Salt Lake City, he won **gold and silver**, despite **a brutal crash and a dramatic photo-finish dive.**

By the end of his career, Ohno had **eight Olympic medals,** making him the most decorated American Winter Olympian ever.

100 MIND-BLOWING OLYMPIC MOMENTS

Mind-Blowing Olympic Moment #62

MIND-BLOWING OLYMPIC MOMENT #62

THE GYMNAST WHO WON GOLD... WITH A TORN ACHILLES

At the **2008 Beijing Olympics**, Chinese gymnast **Li Xiaopeng** faced a nightmare scenario—**a torn Achilles tendon just months before the Games.**

Many thought he wouldn't compete, let alone win. But Xiaopeng **refused to give up**, training through intense pain and adjusting his routines to protect his injury.

When the moment came, he delivered a **flawless parallel bars routine**, scoring an incredible **16.450** to **win gold.**

His comeback made him one of the **greatest gymnasts in history,** with **four Olympic golds and 16 world titles.**

Mind-Blowing Olympic Moment #63

MIND-BLOWING OLYMPIC MOMENT #63

THE WRESTLER WHO WON GOLD... WITH A BROKEN RIB

At the **2012 London Olympics**, Cuban wrestler **Mijaín López** dominated the Greco-Roman wrestling tournament—but what no one knew was that **he was competing with a broken rib.**

Suffering the injury in an earlier match, López **kept his pain a secret, knowing that withdrawing wasn't an option.**

Despite the intense physicality of wrestling, he **crushed every opponent** without conceding a single point, securing **his second Olympic gold.**

He went on to win **five Olympic medals**, cementing his legacy as one of the greatest wrestlers ever.

Mind-Blowing Olympic Moment #64

MIND-BLOWING OLYMPIC MOMENT #64

THE RUNNER WHO WON GOLD... WITH ONE SHOE

At the **1936 Berlin Olympics,** Japanese runner **Shuhei Nishida** lined up for the **5000m final** with a serious disadvantage—**he had lost one of his shoes just before the race.**

Instead of withdrawing, Nishida **wrapped his bare foot in bandages** and decided to race anyway.

Despite running half the race with **one foot on the track and the other wrapped in cloth,** he powered through the pain and **stunned the crowd by winning silver.**

His resilience became a symbol of **true Olympic grit.**

Mind-Blowing Olympic Moment #65

MIND-BLOWING OLYMPIC MOMENT #65

THE ROWERS WHO WON GOLD... WITH ZERO EXPERIENCE

At the **1948 London Olympics**, the **University of California crew team** pulled off one of the greatest upsets in rowing history—**winning gold despite having no international experience.**

Unlike their competitors, who were elite, full-time athletes, the American team consisted of **college students who trained part-time.**

Facing Olympic champions from Britain and Norway, the U.S. crew **powered through rough waters and exhaustion, shocking the world by winning gold.**

Their victory remains one of the greatest underdog stories in Olympic rowing history.

Mind-Blowing Olympic Moment #66

MIND-BLOWING OLYMPIC MOMENT #66

THE MARATHONER WHO WAS ATTACKED MID-RACE

At the **1904 St. Louis Olympics**, Cuban runner **Félix Carvajal** had already overcome incredible odds to compete—**he hitchhiked and ran on foot just to make it to the Games.**

During the marathon, things took a bizarre turn when **he stopped to chat with spectators, ate rotten apples from an orchard, and suffered stomach cramps.**

But the biggest shock? **He was attacked mid-race by a stray dog!**

Despite all this, Carvajal **still finished fourth**, proving that nothing—not even a dog bite—could stop his Olympic dream.

Mind-Blowing Olympic Moment #67

MIND-BLOWING OLYMPIC MOMENT #67

THE GYMNAST WHO WON GOLD... AFTER SURVIVING A WAR

At the **1956 Melbourne Olympics**, Hungarian gymnast **Ágnes Keleti** became a legend—not just for her athleticism, but for her sheer survival.

Born in Hungary, Keleti was preparing for the **1940 Olympics** when World War II broke out. As a **Jewish athlete**, she was forced into hiding, **pretending to be a Christian maid** to escape Nazi persecution.

After the war, she returned to gymnastics stronger than ever. At the 1956 Games, she **won five medals, including four golds,** making her one of the most decorated gymnasts in history.

Her journey from **survival to Olympic glory** remains one of the most inspiring in sports history.

Mind-Blowing Olympic Moment #68

MIND-BLOWING OLYMPIC MOMENT #68

THE SPRINTER WHO WON GOLD... WITH A CIGARETTE IN HIS HAND

At the **1928 Amsterdam Olympics, Percy Williams** stunned the world by winning **gold in both the 100m and 200m sprints**—but what made it truly mind-blowing?

Williams was known for **smoking cigarettes before his races.** While today's athletes follow strict diets and training regimens, Williams casually **lit up a cigarette before stepping onto the track!**

Despite this unorthodox approach, he **blazed past the competition, becoming the fastest man in the world.** His victories remain a legendary example of raw natural talent.

Mind-Blowing Olympic Moment #69

MIND-BLOWING OLYMPIC MOMENT #69

THE SKIER WHO WON GOLD... AFTER BORROWING HIS SKIS

At the **1980 Lake Placid Olympics**, Swedish cross-country skier **Thomas Wassberg** pulled off one of the most dramatic gold medal wins ever—**by just 0.01 seconds.**

But what made it even crazier? **He won with borrowed skis.**

Before the race, Wassberg's own skis weren't gliding well in the icy conditions. So, in a last-minute decision, he **borrowed a teammate's spare pair.**

Despite using unfamiliar skis, he **edged out Finland's Juha Mieto by 0.01 seconds**, marking the closest finish in Olympic skiing history.

After that race, Olympic timing rules were changed—**finishes can no longer be decided by just 0.01 seconds.**

100 MIND-BLOWING OLYMPIC MOMENTS

Mind-Blowing Olympic Moment #70

MIND-BLOWING OLYMPIC MOMENT #70

THE BOXER WHO WON GOLD... WHILE NEARLY BLIND

At the **1908 London Olympics**, American boxer **John Douglas** won gold—but what most people didn't know was that he was **almost completely blind in one eye.**

A childhood accident had left him with **severely impaired vision,** but he never told anyone, fearing he wouldn't be allowed to compete.

Despite this huge disadvantage, Douglas **fought through every round and won gold**, becoming one of the most unlikely champions in Olympic history.

His story remains a testament to **fighting spirit—literally.**

Mind-Blowing Olympic Moment #71

MIND-BLOWING OLYMPIC MOMENT #71

SETTING A WORLD RECORD... WITH A DISLOCATED ELBOW

At the **1972 Munich Olympics**, Soviet weightlifter **Vasily Alekseyev** was attempting to set a **world record in the clean and jerk**—when disaster struck.

On his second lift, his **elbow partially dislocated under the massive weight.** Most athletes would have immediately withdrawn.

Instead, Alekseyev **shook off the pain, reset himself, and successfully lifted a record-breaking 256 kg (564 lbs) on his final attempt.**

His toughness made him one of the most dominant Olympic weightlifters in history, winning **two gold medals and breaking 80 world records.**

: Mind-Blowing Olympic Moment #72

MIND-BLOWING OLYMPIC MOMENT #72

THE RUNNER WHO WON GOLD... AFTER BEING DEAD LAST

At the **1964 Tokyo Olympics, Billy Mills,** an unknown Native American runner from the U.S., pulled off one of the greatest upsets in Olympic history in the **10,000m final.**

With one lap to go, Mills was **trapped in third place, far behind the leaders.** No one expected him to win.

But in the final stretch, **he found another gear, surged past the favorites, and crossed the finish line in complete disbelief.**

Mills remains the **only American to ever win Olympic gold in the 10,000m.** His unexpected victory is still considered one of the greatest moments in distance running.

Mind-Blowing Olympic Moment #73

MIND-BLOWING OLYMPIC MOMENT #73

THE SWIMMER WHO WON GOLD... AFTER BREAKING HIS ARM

At the **1956 Melbourne Olympics**, Australian swimmer **Murray Rose** stunned the world by winning **three gold medals**—but what made it even more unbelievable?

He had broken his arm just months before the Games.

Doctors told him he wouldn't recover in time, but Rose refused to accept that. He **trained through the pain, adjusted his stroke, and defied the odds.**

By the time he hit the water in Melbourne, he **dominated the 400m freestyle, 1500m freestyle, and 4x200m relay**, cementing himself as one of the greatest Olympic swimmers ever.

Mind-Blowing Olympic Moment #74

MIND-BLOWING OLYMPIC MOMENT #74

WINNING GOLD... AFTER BEING CARRIED OFF ON A STRETCHER

At the **1996 Atlanta Olympics**, American gymnast **Kerri Strug** delivered one of the most heroic performances in Olympic history.

In the **team final**, the U.S. needed a strong vault to secure gold. On her first attempt, Strug **landed awkwardly and tore ligaments in her ankle**.

With the pressure on, she **limped back for one last attempt**. Despite the pain, she **stuck the landing on one foot** before collapsing in agony.

She had done enough—the U.S. won its **first-ever Olympic gold in women's gymnastics**. Moments later, she was **carried off on a stretcher, forever a legend**.

100 MIND-BLOWING OLYMPIC MOMENTS

Mind-Blowing Olympic Moment #75

MIND-BLOWING OLYMPIC MOMENT #75

THE BOXER WHO WON GOLD... WITH A BROKEN JAW

At the **1976 Montreal Olympics**, American boxer **Howard Davis Jr.** faced a heartbreaking situation—**his mother passed away just days before his first fight.**

Devastated but determined to honor her, Davis fought through the tournament, winning every match. In the final, he suffered a **broken jaw early in the bout**—but **kept fighting through the pain.**

Despite the injury, Davis **outclassed his opponent and won gold, dedicating the victory to his mother.** He was later voted the tournament's **Most Outstanding Boxer**—even over the great Sugar Ray Leonard.

100 MIND-BLOWING OLYMPIC MOMENTS

Mind-Blowing Olympic Moment #76

MIND-BLOWING OLYMPIC MOMENT #76

THE RUNNER WHO FINISHED THE RACE... ON ONE LEG

At the **1968 Mexico City Olympics**, Tanzanian marathon runner **John Stephen Akhwari** suffered a brutal fall early in the race, **dislocating his knee and tearing a ligament.**

Most athletes would have quit—but Akhwari refused.

Limping and staggering in pain, he **continued running for over 10 miles, long after the race was over.**

Over an hour after the winner had finished, he **hobbled into the stadium to a standing ovation** and crossed the finish line.

When asked why he didn't quit, he simply said: "My country didn't send me 5,000 miles to start the race. They sent me to finish it."

100 MIND-BLOWING OLYMPIC MOMENTS

Mind-Blowing Olympic Moment #77

MIND-BLOWING OLYMPIC MOMENT #77

THE SKIER WHO WON GOLD... WITHOUT SEEING THE COURSE

At the **1984 Sarajevo Olympics**, American skier **Bill Johnson** shocked the world by **becoming the first American to win downhill skiing gold.**

What made it mind-blowing? **He never skied the full course before the race.**

Due to heavy snowfall, the final practice run was canceled, meaning Johnson had to **race the course blind**, relying only on video footage and instinct.

Despite this, he **attacked the mountain at full speed** and crossed the finish line as the fastest man on the slope, forever changing the perception of American skiing.

100 MIND-BLOWING OLYMPIC MOMENTS

Mind-Blowing Olympic Moment #78

MIND-BLOWING OLYMPIC MOMENT #78

THE ARCHER WHO SHOT A PERFECT BULLSEYE... BLINDFOLDED

At the **1976 Montreal Olympics**, South Korean archer **Kim Soo-Nyung** stunned the world during a practice demonstration by **hitting a perfect bullseye while blindfolded.**

The Olympic champion was known for her **unbelievable accuracy**, but when challenged to **shoot without sight**, she calmly drew her bow and landed the arrow dead center.

Though it wasn't part of official competition, the jaw-dropping feat became legendary, proving that **true mastery is about skill, not just sight.**

Mind-Blowing Olympic Moment #79

MIND-BLOWING OLYMPIC MOMENT #79

THE WEIGHTLIFTER WHO SET A WORLD RECORD... THEN FAINTED

At the **1988 Seoul Olympics,** Bulgarian weightlifter **Stefan Topurov** attempted a **world-record clean and jerk in the lightweight category.**

With the crowd on edge, he **hoisted the massive barbell overhead,** locking it in place—**but as soon as the judges gave the signal, he collapsed unconscious.**

The weight had drained him so completely that his body **shut down on the spot.** Officials rushed to revive him, and moments later, he **woke up to the news that he had set a new Olympic record!**

It was a display of **unmatched strength—and absolute exhaustion.**

100 MIND-BLOWING OLYMPIC MOMENTS

Mind-Blowing Olympic Moment #80

MIND-BLOWING OLYMPIC MOMENT #80

THE RUNNER WHO WON GOLD... AFTER STUMBLING AT THE START

At the **2008 Beijing Olympics**, Jamaican sprinter **Usain Bolt** was already the fastest man on Earth—but in the **100m final**, he didn't have a perfect start.

Just **a few steps in, he stumbled slightly**, losing precious milliseconds. Most runners would have panicked—but not Bolt.

Instead, he **exploded with unbelievable speed**, pulling ahead by such a massive margin that he **started celebrating before crossing the finish line.**

Despite slowing down at the end, he **still broke the world record (9.69 seconds)**—a time he would later shatter again. His victory cemented him as **the greatest sprinter of all time.**

…

Mind-Blowing Olympic Moment #81

MIND-BLOWING OLYMPIC MOMENT #81

THE CYCLIST WHO WON GOLD... AFTER A MID-RACE CRASH

At the **2012 London Olympics**, British cyclist **Victoria Pendleton** was chasing gold in the women's keirin final when disaster struck—**she crashed in an earlier round.**

Most riders would have been shaken, but Pendleton **got back on her bike, won her next race, and advanced to the final.**

In the gold medal race, she **timed her sprint perfectly,** surging ahead in the last moments to **win Olympic gold in her final race before retirement.**

Her comeback made her one of the most celebrated cyclists in British history.

Mind-Blowing Olympic Moment #82

MIND-BLOWING OLYMPIC MOMENT #82

THE WRESTLER WHO WON GOLD... IN JUST 11 SECONDS

At the **1936 Berlin Olympics**, Swedish wrestler **Ivar Johansson** pulled off one of the fastest victories in Olympic history—**winning his gold medal match in just 11 seconds.**

Facing a strong opponent in the **Greco-Roman welterweight final**, Johansson **executed a perfect move right at the whistle, pinning his rival instantly.**

Before most spectators had even settled into their seats, the match was over—and Johansson had **claimed his second Olympic gold.**

His lightning-fast win remains one of the **quickest gold-medal victories ever.**

100 MIND-BLOWING OLYMPIC MOMENTS

Mind-Blowing Olympic Moment #83

MIND-BLOWING OLYMPIC MOMENT #83

THE RUNNER WHO LOST HIS SHOE... AND STILL WON SILVER

At the **1932 Los Angeles Olympics**, American middle-distance runner **Glenn Cunningham** lined up for the **1500m final**, unaware that his race would become legendary.

Just a few strides in, **another runner accidentally stepped on his foot, ripping his shoe clean off.**

Most athletes would have stopped—but Cunningham **kept running, barefoot on one foot.** Despite the pain, he **powered through and finished second, winning Olympic silver.**

His determination made him a **fan favorite** and one of the toughest runners of his time.

Mind-Blowing Olympic Moment #84

MIND-BLOWING OLYMPIC MOMENT #84

THE SHOOTER WHO WON GOLD... AFTER BEING NEARLY PARALYZED

At the **1976 Montreal Olympics**, Soviet shooter **Alexander Karpov** overcame a life-changing injury to claim Olympic glory.

Years before the Games, **a severe spinal injury left him partially paralyzed**, and doctors told him he might never walk again—let alone compete.

Refusing to accept that fate, Karpov **underwent years of grueling rehabilitation**, retraining his body and perfecting his shooting technique despite his limitations.

When the Olympics arrived, he **stunned the world by winning gold in the 50m rifle event**, proving that mental strength can overcome any obstacle.

Mind-Blowing Olympic Moment #85

MIND-BLOWING OLYMPIC MOMENT #85

THE SKIER WHO WON GOLD... AFTER BREAKING HIS BACK

At the **1998 Nagano Olympics**, Austrian skier **Hermann Maier** delivered one of the most legendary comebacks in Olympic history.

Just months before the Games, Maier **crashed violently during a training run, breaking his back.** Doctors told him he might never compete again.

But Maier refused to quit. After an intense recovery, he **not only made it to the Olympics—but dominated the slopes**, winning **gold in both the super-G and giant slalom.**

His comeback earned him the nickname **"The Herminator"** and solidified his place as one of the greatest skiers ever.

Mind-Blowing Olympic Moment #86

MIND-BLOWING OLYMPIC MOMENT #86

THE MARATHON RUNNER WHO GOT LOST... AND STILL WON

At the **1908 London Olympics**, Italian runner **Dorando Pietri** was on track to win the **marathon**, but with just a few miles left, **he made a wrong turn.**

Disoriented and exhausted, Pietri ran in the **wrong direction**, costing himself valuable time before officials redirected him.

When he finally entered the stadium for the final lap, **he collapsed multiple times**, needing help just to stay on his feet.

Though he was disqualified for receiving assistance, **his courage captured the world's heart**, and he was later awarded a special trophy by Queen Alexandra.

Mind-Blowing Olympic Moment #87

MIND-BLOWING OLYMPIC MOMENT #87

THE BOBSLEDDER WHO WON GOLD... AFTER TRACK AND FIELD

At the **2002 Salt Lake City Olympics**, American athlete **Vonetta Flowers** made history—not as a sprinter, but as a **bobsledder.**

Originally a track and field star, Flowers **missed qualifying for the Summer Olympics** and nearly retired. But when she got the chance to try **bobsledding—a sport she had never competed in before—she took the leap.**

Just two years later, she **won gold in the two-woman bobsled event,** becoming the **first Black athlete to win Winter Olympic gold.**

Her incredible journey proved that sometimes, **the right path isn't the one you planned.**

100 MIND-BLOWING OLYMPIC MOMENTS

Mind-Blowing Olympic Moment #88

MIND-BLOWING OLYMPIC MOMENT #88

WINNING GOLD... AFTER NEARLY DROWNING AS A CHILD

At the **1932 Los Angeles Olympics**, Japanese swimmer **Yasuji Miyazaki** became an Olympic champion—but few knew that years earlier, he had **nearly drowned as a child.**

Terrified of the water after the incident, his parents **forced him to take swimming lessons to overcome his fear.**

Not only did he conquer his fear—he went on to **win gold in the 100m freestyle** at just **15 years old,** making him the **youngest male Olympic swimming champion ever.**

His story is a testament to **turning fear into greatness.**

Mind-Blowing Olympic Moment #89

MIND-BLOWING OLYMPIC MOMENT #89

THE RUNNER WHO WON GOLD... WITH A HEART CONDITION

At the **1964 Tokyo Olympics**, Kenyan runner **Kip Keino** became a legend—not just for winning, but for **doing it while battling a severe heart condition.**

Doctors warned him **not to compete** due to a chronic heart ailment, but Keino refused to quit.

In the **1500m final**, he outran the favorite, **Jim Ryun, by an astonishing 20 meters**—one of the largest margins in Olympic history.

His perseverance made him **one of Kenya's greatest distance runners** and inspired future generations of athletes.

100 MIND-BLOWING OLYMPIC MOMENTS

Mind-Blowing Olympic Moment #90

MIND-BLOWING OLYMPIC MOMENT #90

THE SKIER WHO WON GOLD... AFTER CRASHING MID-RACE

At the **1998 Nagano Olympics**, Norwegian skier **Bjørn Dæhlie** proved why he was one of the greatest cross-country skiers of all time.

In the **50km race**, Dæhlie was leading when he **took a brutal fall on an icy downhill section.** Most skiers would have lost all momentum—but not him.

He **jumped back up, powered through the remaining kilometers, and still won gold**—his record-breaking **eighth Olympic gold medal.**

His resilience cemented him as one of the **greatest Winter Olympians ever.**

Mind-Blowing Olympic Moment #91

MIND-BLOWING OLYMPIC MOMENT #91

THE WEIGHTLIFTER WHO WON GOLD... AT 17 YEARS OLD

At the **2000 Sydney Olympics**, Greek weightlifter **Pyrros Dimas** became a legend by **winning his third consecutive Olympic gold.**

But what many forget is that he started his Olympic career as a **teenager—winning his first gold at just 17 years old.**

Despite facing seasoned champions, Dimas **dominated his category and lifted his way into history.**

His legacy made him one of the **greatest Olympic weightlifters of all time.**

Mind-Blowing Olympic Moment #92

MIND-BLOWING OLYMPIC MOMENT #92

THE SPRINTER WHO WON GOLD... WITH NO ACLS

At the **2008 Beijing Olympics,** American sprinter **LaShawn Merritt** shocked the world by dominating the **400m final**—but what no one knew?

He was born without ACLs in both knees.

The anterior cruciate ligament (ACL) is crucial for stability, yet Merritt **never had them from birth**—a condition that would have ended most athletic careers before they started.

Instead, he **blew past the competition to win Olympic gold,** proving that sometimes, **the body can adapt in ways science can't explain.**

Mind-Blowing Olympic Moment #93

MIND-BLOWING OLYMPIC MOMENT #93

THE SKIER WHO WON GOLD... AFTER SLEEPING IN A BARN

At the **1960 Squaw Valley Olympics**, French skier **Jean Vuarnet** wasn't just racing against the competition—he was racing against exhaustion.

Due to **overbooked accommodations**, Vuarnet **had to sleep in a barn** the night before the downhill skiing final.

Despite the lack of rest, he **dominated the slopes the next morning and won gold.** Even more incredible? He did it using **a brand-new technique—tucking in a low aerodynamic stance, now known as the "egg position."**

His victory changed ski racing forever.

100 MIND-BLOWING OLYMPIC MOMENTS

Mind-Blowing Olympic Moment #94

MIND-BLOWING OLYMPIC MOMENT #94

WINNING GOLD... AFTER MISSING THE OLYMPICS TWICE

At the **1992 Barcelona Olympics**, Belarusian gymnast **Vitaly Scherbo** made history by winning **six gold medals**—the most ever in a single Games for a gymnast.

But what made his dominance even more incredible? **He had missed two previous Olympics due to political turmoil.**

Originally from the Soviet Union, Scherbo **was supposed to compete in 1988, but he was too young.** Then, in 1991, **the Soviet Union collapsed**, leaving him without a country.

After finally getting the chance to compete in 1992 under the Unified Team, he delivered one of the **greatest gymnastics performances ever.**

100 MIND-BLOWING OLYMPIC MOMENTS

Mind-Blowing Olympic Moment #95

MIND-BLOWING OLYMPIC MOMENT #95

THE WEIGHTLIFTER WHO WON GOLD... AFTER COLLAPSING MID-LIFT

At the **2008 Beijing Olympics**, German weightlifter **Matthias Steiner** faced the biggest moment of his career—**his final attempt in the super-heavyweight category.**

As he lifted a massive **258kg (569 lbs)**, he suddenly **lost control, and the bar came crashing down on his neck.**

Most thought his competition was over—but Steiner **shook it off, refocused, and came back for his final lift.**

With the pressure on, he **hoisted the weight successfully, winning gold and dedicating his victory to his late wife.**

100 MIND-BLOWING OLYMPIC MOMENTS

Mind-Blowing Olympic Moment #96

MIND-BLOWING OLYMPIC MOMENT #96

THE ROWER WHO WON GOLD... WITH ONE LUNG

At the **1928 Amsterdam Olympics**, British rower **Jack Beresford** made history by **winning gold in the single sculls event.**

What made his victory even more incredible? **He had only one functioning lung.**

After surviving **a near-fatal case of pneumonia as a child,** Beresford was left with severely reduced lung capacity.

Yet, against competitors with full lung power, he powered through the final stretch and **claimed Olympic gold, proving that heart matters more than lungs.**

100 MIND-BLOWING OLYMPIC MOMENTS

Mind-Blowing Olympic Moment #97

MIND-BLOWING OLYMPIC MOMENT #97

THE RUNNER WHO WON GOLD... AFTER BEATING MALARIA

At the **1996 Atlanta Olympics,** Nigerian sprinter **Chioma Ajunwa** made history by winning **gold in the long jump**—but her journey to the top was anything but easy.

Just **months before the Games,** Ajunwa was diagnosed with **malaria,** an illness that left her bedridden and weak. Many thought her Olympic dreams were over.

But she **fought back, trained relentlessly, and delivered a stunning performance,** becoming the **first African woman to win Olympic gold in a field event.**

Her victory was a triumph of **grit over adversity.**

100 MIND-BLOWING OLYMPIC MOMENTS

Mind-Blowing Olympic Moment #98

MIND-BLOWING OLYMPIC MOMENT #98

THE WRESTLER WHO WON GOLD... AFTER BEING KNOCKED OUT

At the **2000 Sydney Olympics**, Russian Greco-Roman wrestler **Rulon Gardner** pulled off one of the greatest upsets in Olympic history—but not before getting knocked out.

Facing the undefeated **Aleksandr Karelin**, a three-time Olympic champion who hadn't lost a match in 13 years, Gardner was a massive underdog.

Early in the match, **he took a brutal hit that briefly knocked him unconscious**—but instead of quitting, he **got back up and stunned the world by defeating Karelin for the gold.**

His victory is still considered one of the **biggest shocks in Olympic history.**

100 MIND-BLOWING OLYMPIC MOMENTS

Mind-Blowing Olympic Moment #99

MIND-BLOWING OLYMPIC MOMENT #99

THE GYMNAST WHO WON GOLD... AFTER A WAR INJURY

At the **1948 London Olympics**, Czechoslovakian gymnast **Vera Růžičková** overcame unimaginable odds to win gold—**just years after suffering a serious war injury.**

During World War II, Růžičková was **injured in a bombing raid**, leaving her with permanent scars and doubts about ever competing again.

But she refused to let that stop her. Training in **post-war poverty with limited resources**, she made it to the Olympics and **led Czechoslovakia to team gold in gymnastics**.

Her victory was a symbol of **resilience and strength in the face of adversity.**

Mind-Blowing Olympic Moment #100

MIND-BLOWING OLYMPIC MOMENT #100

THE SWIMMER WHO WON GOLD... WITH A STOMACH VIRUS

At the **2012 London Olympics**, American swimmer **Dana Vollmer** wasn't just battling the competition—**she was battling a severe stomach virus.**

Feeling weak and nauseous before the **100m butterfly final**, Vollmer had every reason to doubt herself. But instead of withdrawing, she **fought through the pain, dove into the pool, and delivered the swim of her life.**

Not only did she **win gold**, but she **set a new world record**, touching the wall in **55.98 seconds**.

Her grit and resilience turned what could have been a disaster into **one of the greatest performances in Olympic swimming history.**

CONCLUSION

Congratulations! You've just explored **100 of the most mind-blowing Olympic moments**—stories of **unbelievable triumph, wild surprises, and record-shattering feats** that prove why the Olympics are **the greatest stage in sports.**

But here's the thing about the Olympics—**they're never finished.** For every jaw-dropping moment in this book, **there are countless more waiting to be made.** New athletes will rise, new records will fall, and the next generation of competitors will redefine what's possible.

Maybe this book has reignited your passion for the Games, or perhaps it's given you a whole new appreciation for **the dedication, drama, and sheer unpredictability** of Olympic history. Either way, one thing is certain—**the Olympic spirit is unstoppable.**

As you close this book, don't think of it as the finish line. **Think of it as the starting block for**

your next journey of discovery. The Olympics will continue to amaze, inspire, and push the limits of human potential.

Until next time, stay curious, stay inspired, and remember: **the greatest Olympic moments are the ones still waiting to be written.**

ACKNOWLEDGEMENTS

Creating *100 Mind-Blowing Olympic Moments* has been a journey filled with passion, inspiration, and a deep appreciation for the incredible athletes who make the Olympic Games so unforgettable. While my name may be on the cover, this book wouldn't exist without the support, encouragement, and stories shared by so many amazing people.

First, a heartfelt thank you to **the athletes, historians, and sports fans** who have kept these Olympic moments alive. Your love for the Games and the legendary stories they produce have been a constant source of inspiration. This book is a tribute to the incredible history you've helped uncover.

To my **family and friends**, who patiently listened as I marveled at jaw-dropping Olympic feats—thank you for your endless support (and for pretending to be just as fascinated as I was). Your encouragement kept me going every step of the way.

A huge shoutout to **you—the reader!** Whether you came here for the record-breaking moments, the wild surprises, or just a little Olympic trivia to impress your friends, this book is for you. Your curiosity and appreciation for the Olympic spirit are what keep these stories alive.

And finally, to the **Olympic Games themselves**—thank you for being the ultimate showcase of human potential, perseverance, and greatness. You have given the world moments that inspire, unite, and remind us that **nothing is impossible.**

Here's to the Olympics, to the stories yet to be written, and to the extraordinary athletes who continue to push the limits of what we believe is possible.

ABOUT THE AUTHOR

Felix Grayson is a storyteller at heart, driven by an insatiable curiosity for the **strange, surprising, and downright unpredictable moments in sports.** With a passion for uncovering the wildest and most unbelievable tales from the **Olympic Games**, Felix has crafted *100 Mind-Blowing Olympic Moments* to **entertain, amaze, and spark wonder in fans of all ages.**

When he's not digging through archives or chasing down the next **jaw-dropping Olympic feat,** Felix enjoys **watching replays of history-making performances, exploring the stories behind sports legends, and pondering life's most fascinating questions over a cup of coffee.** A firm believer in the magic of the Olympics and the power of a great story, Felix invites you to take this journey through the **most mind-blowing moments in Olympic history,** proving that the Games are just as full of surprises as they are of champions.

www.ingramcontent.com/pod-product-compliance
Lightning Source LLC
Chambersburg PA
CBHW030318080526
44584CB00012B/618